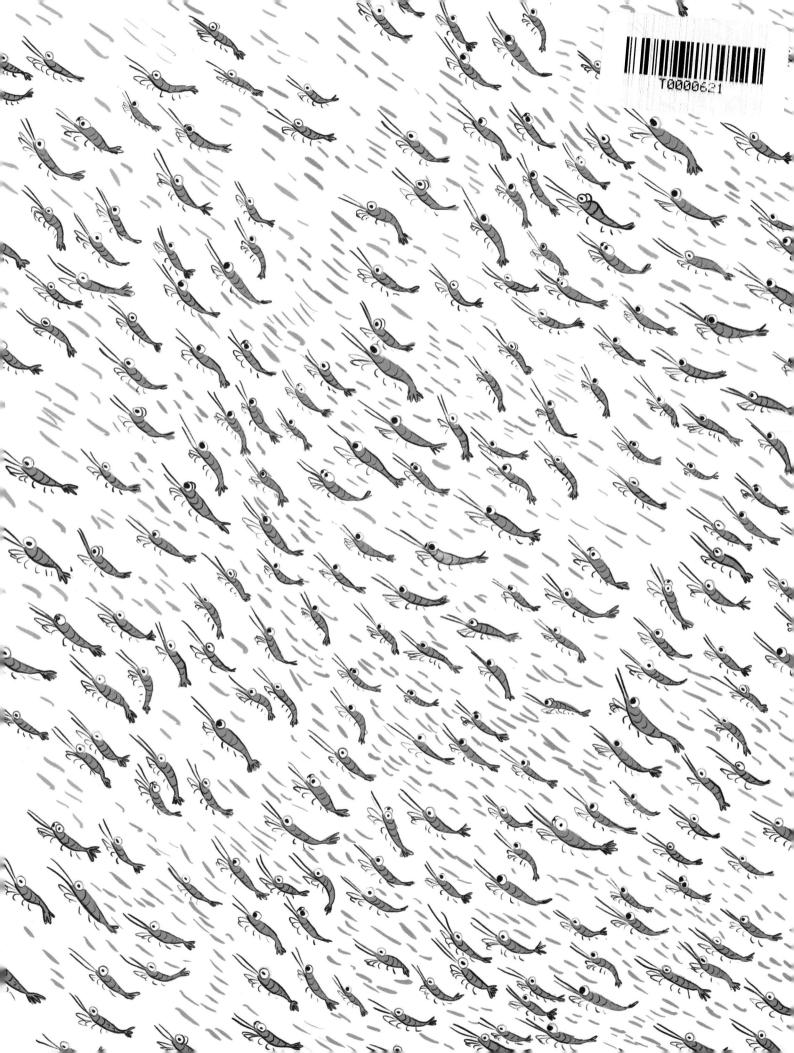

# GOOD EATING

### The ^short Life of Krill

Written by
**Matt Lilley**

Illustrated by
**Dan Tavis**

TILBURY HOUSE PUBLISHERS

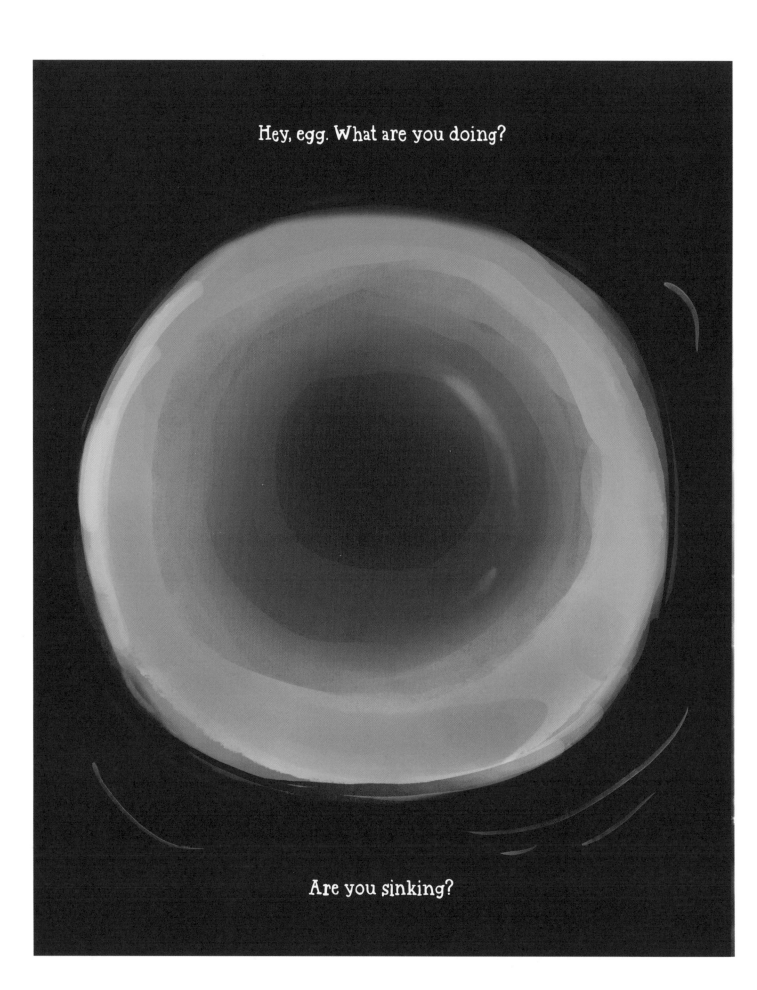

A sinking egg....

For many days, you sink.

You sink a mile down, and

you keep going down...

down...

until...

You wiggle . . .

You stretch . . . You push . . .

You hatch!

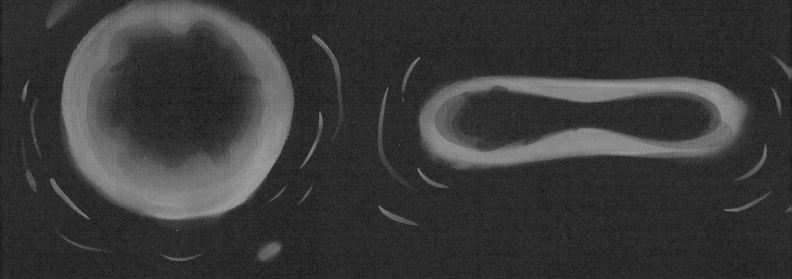

You're not an egg anymore.

You're kind of a sphere.

After a while, you grow into . . .

. . . kind of an oval.

Are those arms?

You are a six-armed oval.

You grow pokey spines.

But what are you?

*nauplius (NAW-plee-us)*

What are you doing now?

You swim up a bit, then rest. Up. Then rest.

For your new body, you grow a new shell. After a few
weeks, this shell breaks apart and you come out . . .

*metanauplius*
*(MET–uh–NAW–plee–us)*

. . . changed. You grow more spines.

But now what are you?

You still have no mouth. Aren't you getting hungry?

Maybe you're not hungry yet, but those fish down
there look hungry. What do they eat?

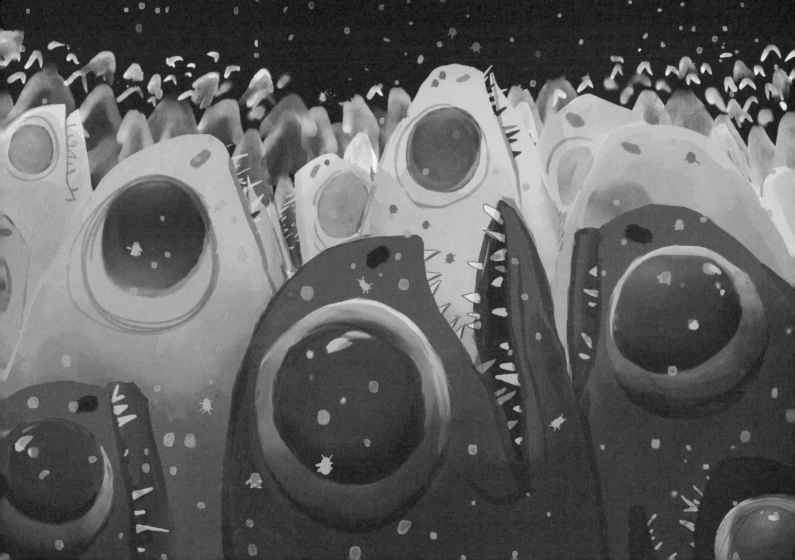

Better not think about that! Just keep swimming, up, up, up.

And growing.

For your new body,
you grow a new shell.

How are you doing all this
growing without eating?

And are you breaking
out of your shell again?
It sure looks like you are . . .

Your shell breaks apart
again, and you come out . . .

...changed. You grow a face...
sort of. About time!

*calyptopsis (CAH-lip-TOP-sis)*

You have two eyes now. And
a mouth. And to go with
your new mouth,
a stomach!

Splash! You've reached the surface.

In about four weeks you swam almost two miles up. Now you are hungry!

What are you hungry for? Any plant or animal small enough to fit into that new mouth of yours.

Glub, glub, glub!

You eat all the smallest things. You eat, eat, eat and swim, swim, swim and grow. You grow another new shell. Then you eat-grow-swim and swim-grow-eat.

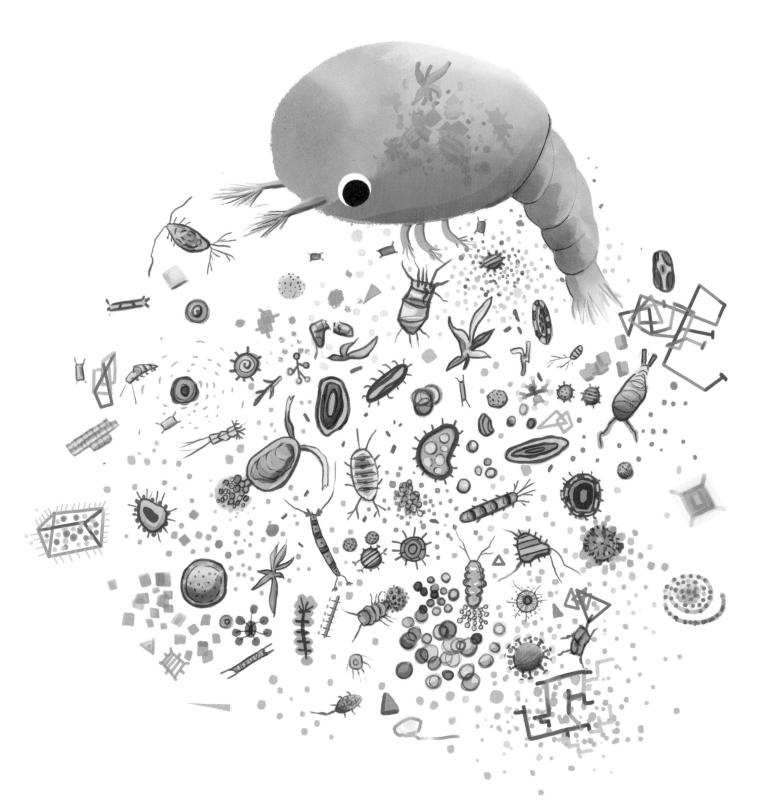

This is what you're good at. Is there anything *else* that you do?

Watch out! Penguins!

What are they looking at? Oh ... You've done such a good job eating that your stomach looks green. You're kind of standing out in the crowd.

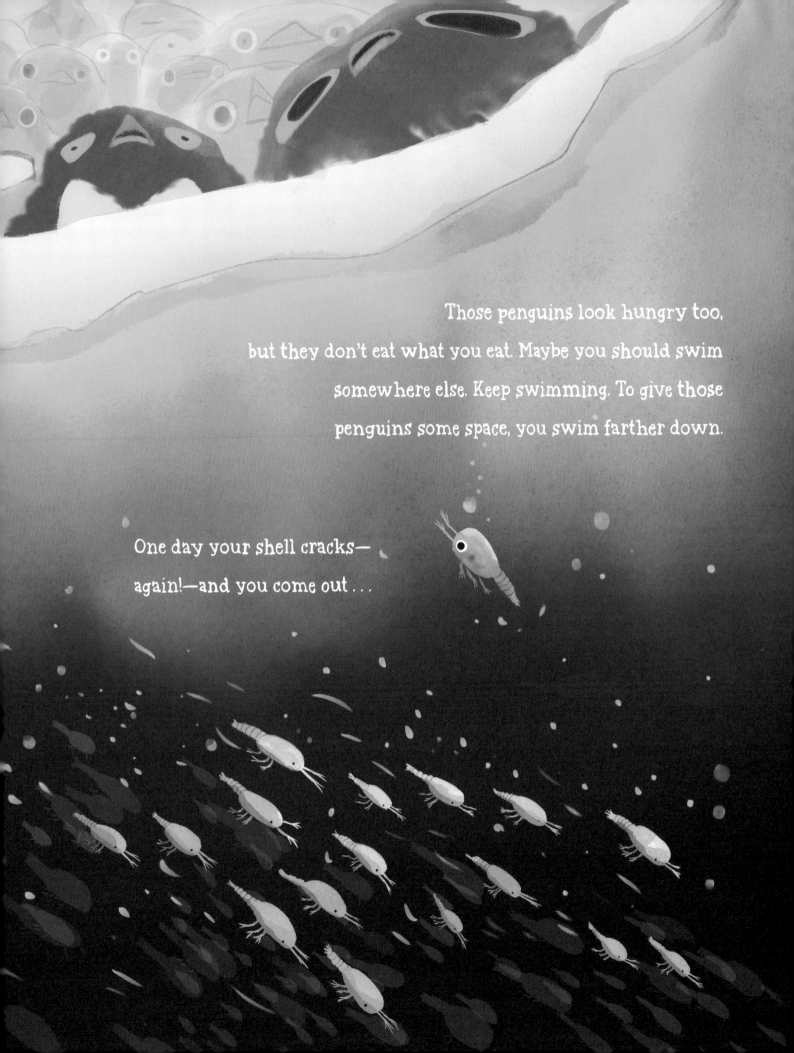

Those penguins look hungry too,
but they don't eat what you eat. Maybe you should swim
somewhere else. Keep swimming. To give those
penguins some space, you swim farther down.

One day your shell cracks—
again!—and you come out . . .

...changed.

furcilia (fur-SIL-ee-uh)

Your eyes are sticking out. You're getting more legs there...

nice!

What have you turned into this time, and what will you do now?

Swim, swim, swim. You weigh more than water, which means, if you stop swimming, you sink.

So you almost Never. Stop. Swimming.

You look kind of buggy, but you're not a bug.

You look kind of shrimpy, but you're not a shrimp.

You are a . . .

... krill!

You swim and eat, eat and swim.

And grow.

Do what you're good at.

Over many weeks, you crack out of your shell
a few more times—doesn't that ever get old?—
until you're almost full-grown.

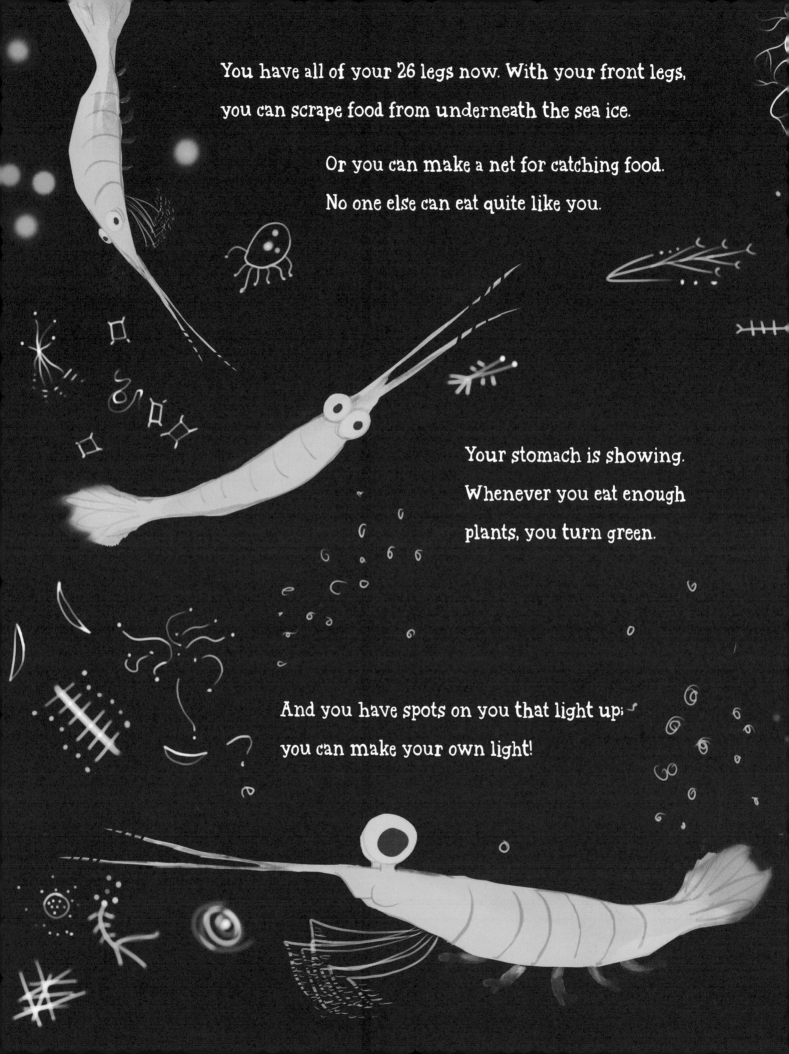

You have all of your 26 legs now. With your front legs,
you can scrape food from underneath the sea ice.

Or you can make a net for catching food.
No one else can eat quite like you.

Your stomach is showing.
Whenever you eat enough
plants, you turn green.

And you have spots on you that light up;
you can make your own light!

And look, there are tons of krill just like you.

There are a million. Maybe a million million!

How much is a million million? Let's call it a krillion.

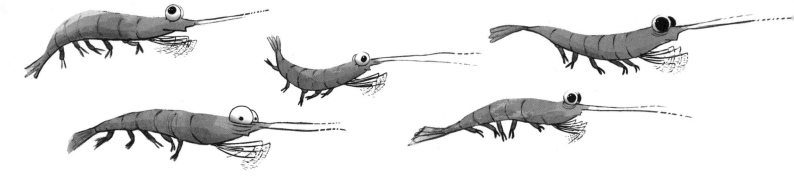

You and your fellow krill are the world's best eaters.

You're all so good at eating, you turned all that tiny food into . . . you.

Watch out, though. There are a lot of other hungry creatures around. When they see you, they see food ... seafood!

On the surface, seabirds swoop down for you.

Under the ice, penguins plunge for you. Down deep, seals might devour you. And then there are the whales ....

Whales are
the world's
biggest creatures.

No one is bigger
than a blue whale. They are
so big, you might think they
only eat big stuff. Actually, blue
whales eat small stuff . . . like you.

I hate to break this to you: You're pretty small yourself, and blue whales
eat stuff your size. Only it takes a lot of you guys to feed a whale.
A million of you might make a meal for one hungry ...

Hey! You got away? You didn't get eaten?

Well then, keep eatin'!

# KRILL: GOOD EATING

Krill are considered the keystone species of the Southern Ocean. That means that of all the life forms in the ocean around Antarctica, krill are the most important. This is because krill are so good at eating. Krill can eat tiny one-celled plants called phytoplankton.

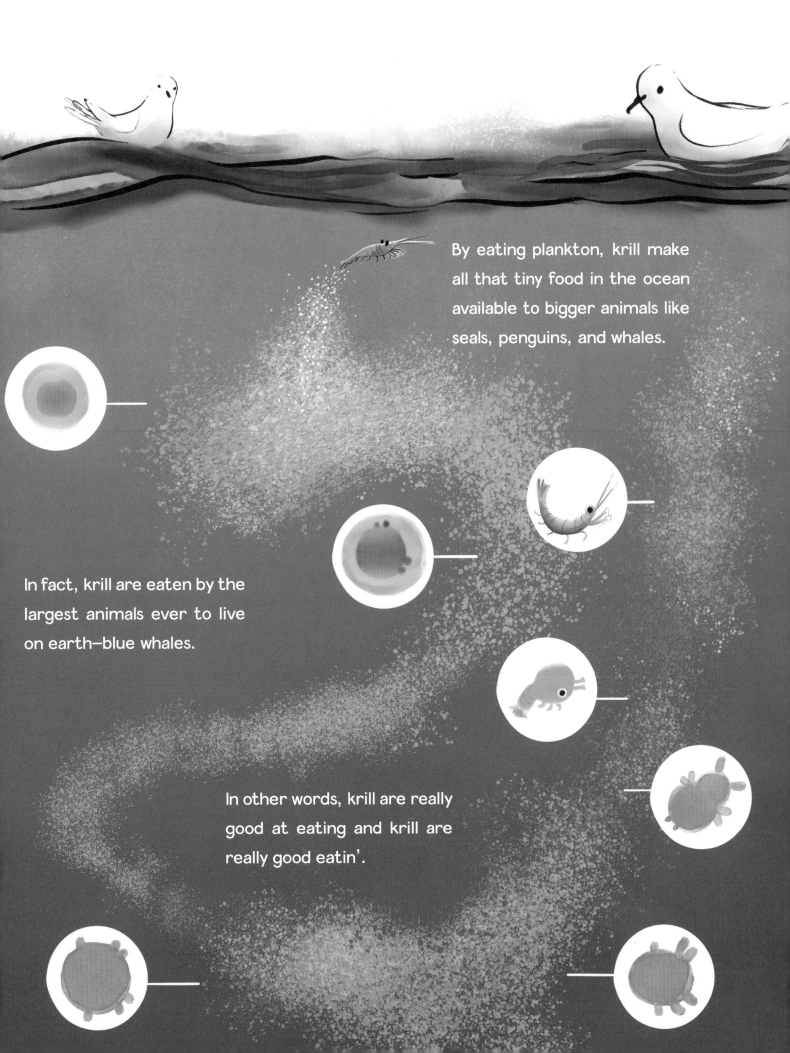

By eating plankton, krill make all that tiny food in the ocean available to bigger animals like seals, penguins, and whales.

In fact, krill are eaten by the largest animals ever to live on earth—blue whales.

In other words, krill are really good at eating and krill are really good eatin'.

# MORE KRILL FACTS

When krill reproduce, the egg-laying females form their own swarm. They swim out past the continental shelf surrounding Antarctica. They swim out to where the water is miles deep. Then they lay their eggs. Their eggs need room to sink. As the eggs sink, the embryos—the unborn krill—develop inside. Then, when the eggs hatch, the larvae—the baby krill—slowly swim back up. As they swim up, they grow, and as they grow, they molt, or shed their shells. Unlike other crustaceans, krill keep right on molting even after they're full-grown.

There are over 80 species of krill in the world. The krill in this book are Antarctic krill (*Euphasia superba*). At about 2.5 inches long, Antarctic krill are among the world's biggest krill, but they're still pretty small.

Krill are bioluminescent. That means they make their own light and can glow at night. Scientists aren't sure why they do this.

A million million is one trillion. Scientists think that there are about 500 trillion krill in the world.

Krill can flip their tails like a lobster to escape a predator, and some scientists even think krill can "molt and bolt," quickly shedding their shells so that an attacking penguin or seabird gets the empty shell decoy while the live krill swims away.

If there's no food around, krill can actually shrink. They don't just get skinnier. They shed their shells and come out smaller. Their survival strategies must work, because krill live up to ten years. That's a short life by human standards but not bad for a small animal in a big ocean.

# LEARNING MORE

**Books**

Batten, Mary, and Thomas Gonzalez. *Life in a Frozen World: Wildlife of Antarctica*. Peachtree Publishing Company Inc., 2020.

Florian, Douglas. *Ice!: Poems about Polar Life*. Holiday House, 2020.

Nicol, Stephen, and Marc Mangel. *The Curious Life of Krill: A Conservation Story from the Bottom of the World*. Island Press, 2018.

Schuh, Mari C. *Blue Whales (Animals)*. Pebble, 2020.

**Online**

Australian Antarctic Program. "Antarctic Krill."
*https://www.antarctica.gov.au/about-antarctica/animals/krill*

LEARNZ. "Antarctic Food Webs."
*https://www.learnz.org.nz/scienceonice144/antarctic-food-webs*

Ward, Paul. "Antarctic Krill - *Euphausia superba* Biology and Adaptations."
*https://coolantarctica.com/Antarctica%20fact%20file/wildlife/krill.php*

**Game**

National Geographic Kids. *Krill Smackdown*.
*https://kids.nationalgeographic.com/games/action-adventure/article/krill-smackdown*

From the website: "Move a group of small, shrimplike animals called krill around the waters off Antarctica. But look out for predators, such as emperor penguins and blue whales, that see these krill as a tasty snack!"

To Tia. I couldn't do this without you. And to Mason and Alexandra. Every day, you inspire me. —M.L.

To my friend and mentor Susan, who guided me through the early artist years. Thank you. —D.T.

**Acknowledgment**
Grateful thanks to Dr. Stephen Nicol, eminent krill biologist and
author of *The Curious Life of Krill*, for his scientific review of this book.

Text © 2022 by Matt Lilley
Illustrations © 2022 by Dan Tavis

Hardcover ISBN 978-0-88448-867-5

Tilbury House Publishers • Thomaston, Maine • www.tilburyhouse.com

Library of Congress Control Number: 2021948049

Designed by Frame25 Productions • Printed in Korea

10 9 8 7 6 5 4 3 2

**Matt Lilley** is a science and technical writer by day with a special emphasis on medical writing for kids. At night he is a children's nonfiction book author, inventing ways to make complicated topics interesting as well as easy to understand. He is also a Minnesota Master Naturalist in his spare time. His previous children's books include *Why We Love* and *Why We Cry* (Capstone) and *Canada Geese* and *Beavers* (in ABDO's "Pond Animals" series). Visit him at mattlilley.ink.

**Dan Tavis** has been doodling since his first math class in elementary school and was inspired to paint upon discovering Bill Watterson's *Calvin and Hobbes* comic strip. Watterson's work remains a major influence. Dan is the illustrator of *Common Critters* (2020), *The Whale Fall Café* (2021), and *Fluffy McWhiskers and the Cuteness Explosion* (2021). Dan creates illustrations with watercolor, ink, and digital media. Visit him at dantavis.com.